Little Ghosts on Castle Floors

Poems informed by the Potterverse

Little Ghosts on Castle Floors

Poems informed by the Potterverse

Wayne-Daniel Berard

Cover design by Shay Culligan
Cover art by Josipa Juras

ISBN: 978-1-63980-147-3

Kelsay Books
502 South 1040 East, A-119
American Fork, Utah 84003
Kelsaybooks.com

For my Christine, in all things.

Introduction and Acknowledgments

There was a time not that long ago when virtually everyone knew their Bible stories and their Greek myths. That time seems to have largely passed.

Today, if I refer to someone as "rich as Croesus," people stare at me blankly.

But should I describe a controversial figure as "He Who Must Not Be Named" or an abusive lover as "a Dementor," almost everyone knowingly nods.

The role that sacred stories and myths once played, that of common cultural language and shared imagery has now largely been taken up by the Harry Potter universe – and widely so! As a dyed-in-the-robe enthusiast, people stop to talk anywhere I go in my Gryffindor scarf or glasses-and-lightning-bolt mask. What house am I in? Who is my favorite character? Have I been to Orlando (the Mecca of this mythos)? It's like belonging to a vast international society, an alternate-universal church!

For a writer or poet, this provides an opportunity and means to communicate through shared layers of depth and delight that many thought had been lost forever. In that spirit, the poems of this chapbook are not *about* Harry Potter; they are formed and informed by the way this magical world can describe and plumb the depths of who we are in the very real here and now.

Like scripture and myth, the Potterverse is a light. This chapbook only seeks to help us once again remember how to turn it on.

—Wayne-Daniel Berard

Infinite thanks to Deborah Liepziger, *Soul-Lit,* Carolyn Martin, Nora Luquer, Emily Rebekah Green, Richard Fox, John McDargh, Judy Cassidy, Trudy Schuman, Tahira Rehman, Delisa Hargrove, Karen Kelsay, and, above all others, my Lovely Christine.

Grateful acknowledgment is made to the following publications in which these poems appeared:

Amethyst Review: "Sorted"

Soul-Lit: "little ghosts on the castle floor," Prisoner of Baskagan," "Havurah Hogwarts"

Contents

there always must be
Children who did not especially want it to happen
—*WH Auden*

"Is that really what my hair looks from the back?"
—*Hermione Granger*

little ghosts on castle floors

Up in the night
when everyone is
sleeping this is
when the poems come
quiet enough to hear
the wind chimes outside
that my hall mates gave
me when my mother passed
they ring in free verse but
wish they weren't the cats
Harry and Albus chase
invisible things like taunting
little ghosts on castle floors
—there's a title—
but this the only time
I can hear my own ears
tinnitus my native tongue
drowned out by the day
the poems come when they're
whistled for the chimes randomly
accentuate syllables and whatever
fun chasing half-existent night
might be I'm having it 1:21 is its
own rhyming couplet and drooping
eyes turn the page cats have managed
their mischief and poem like unpassingness
sings itself again and me to sleep.

After Enlightenment, Then What?

You take a walk down
the bike/walking path
you find you're overdressed
(warmer outside than in) you
leave your jacket on the bench
with your Harry Potter
sunglasses case in its pocket
clusters of wisteria have just
arrived like children of Dionysus
and Vera Ashley every person
greets you especially the dogs
the electric bike plays Born
to Be Wild as it hums past
the jacket and case are
still there when you walk back
and the
sky is hung with candles.

Living Diagon-ally

Notice, the signs
change their names
from mundane to
magical in the presence
I walk down my main
street the window of
Towne News shows
Have You Seen This
Wizard? with my own
smiling face the pole
at Stan's Barber Shop
spins like Weasleys' Wildfire
Whiz-Bangs and Bank of
America drive thru asks
Lamp, please? Key, please?
Can you see it? No
matter. Come join my
friends and me at
at Dunkin' Cauldron,
butter-beer latte awaits!

Express

My poems all have the
same name the same
engine take a seat
check out the table
of contents *(anything
from the trolley, dears?)*
don't worry about the
open windows my
lines have more than
one good jump in them
let your sight be repaired
and scars giggled over
robe yourself in imagery
we'll be arriving soon
the lantern waves itself
(that's how you know) my
poems have all the same
engine The (your name here)
Express.

Goblet of Tired

What I want to know is
Who put my name
in that goddamn cup?
Already underwater
past nest-eggs living
a labyrinthine life who
would do this? And
how many "spares"
left behind along the way?
Never wanted to compete
what dark cloud
what curse follows
chapter to chapter?
Who knows?
But whatever gold
comes of all this
I'll give to Wizards
Wheezes enable
Love Potions Extendable
Ears Pygmy Puffs out
of suffering will come
new dress robes for
best friends who
stay beyond sinking
ships and escaping
carriages who spare
nothing.

Mirror

"All I see is myself,
the way I am now,"
I said. Dumbledore
(the Richard Harris
one not the stupid-
beard-ring one) just
stared into Erised. It
didn't stare back.
"Try mine," I offered
the flip view on my
iphone camera. "It's
called the Mirror of
TahwtheKcuf."

Magic-Borne

Were I on staff at
Hogwarts I'd propose
a new course a counter-
point to Defense Against
the Dark,
Acceptance of
the Light Arts
Picture it! Energy healing
in the Great Hall Reiki as a
Room of Requirement the
Mirror of Past-Life Regression,
just imagine cleansing Severus'
Svadhisthana Ancestral Healing
for You Know Who how cruciatting
to be without all this! How magic-
borne we Muggles after all!

Tao of Wizardry

Harm bounces
off of good because
of love but doesn't
leave it at that
goodness melds
itself with its opposite
no two but one
and each can see
with the other's eyes
He Who Must Not Be
and He Who Can't
Help But Be share
the same soul and
every page thereafter
is One *the Tao*
doesn't take sides
it gives birth to both
good and evil the Kings
Cross that can be described
in words is not the true station

(Italics: *Tao Te Ching, Canto 5*)

Havurah Hogwarts

Too busy sorting
Half-Bloods from Pure-
Bloods from Mud-Bloods
to even notice we J-Bloods.
Good.
We gather Friday nights
in the Room of Requirenot no
houses only *how lovely is your
house, oh*
minyan all the magic
we need we light candles by
quoting: *Vay h'cheyn* and we
hear.
We leave behind the week
of bindings, fear of either-or
night-or-light. We understand.
How often have we faced dark
lords?
unsurprised their every
spell is latin but the killing curse's
aramaic
only when *havdalah* ends
do we raise a wand toward one another
and gently say *Alohamora*

The Borrow

And this is why
to any student who
crosses my door with
"my cupboard under
the stairs, that lead
to my mother's boyfriend"
who hears "freak" "abnormal"
"you've nowhere to go" I
say there's a clock in our
kitchen, my wife's and mine,
with your spoon on it, my
Smart car can't fly but
it can outrun overfed
cruelties and feralness
disguised as family there's
a sweater with your initial
knitting itself you don't
have to earn it come to
think of it we're all rubber
ducks here you can sort
out your priorities no
windows barred an
invitation not a subpoena.
It's not much, but we call
it *The Borrrow* feel free
to.

Prisoner of Baskagan

you are the opposite
of Dementor you breathe
soul into me and I
am magic to my core
forget about dark
robes those scarlett
slacks and grey vee
necks are spellbinding
lean in watch all the
frost ferns in my window
melt to clarity I know
you, magical creature,
Ascentor, Well-Meantor,
Iridescentor.

Love Forgets What It Needs to Forget

She reaches across
my soul and whispers
"Obliviate"
it all vanishes
the give away, the disappointed
adoption, knives of neighborhood,
absolute zero, glacial contempt
gone just like that
You really are the smartest wife of your age.

Application

Don't have gallons
of galleons? Not to
worry. There are
scholarships several
in fact each house:
for the beatifically
ballsy, the consistently
kind, the defiantly brilliant
(despite schoolyard blowback),
the unapologetically thus.
Unsorted? There's the
Shunpike Stranded Fund
(very popular) Dobby
Memorial Award for the
Insistently Free the
AWPB Trust (no one
understands that one
it just happens) Apply?
all you truly need just
shows up magical
abundance don't
believe it? You're
holding this poem,
aren't you?

Poem 9 3/4

How long did we
butt our head
against the brick
wall? Forever?
Before we realized
it's levio-*here,* not
levio-*far* this is our
platform all along
there's our train
countrysides glide
by while we stay
serenely still
(that's the spell)
Hagrid was mistaken
it *is* every day we
turn eleven the bricks
never wanted to
leave us out just
keep us in
despite what
your therapist says,
just because it's happening
outside our head doesn't
mean it isn't real.

Weren't

The dentists
welcomed their
magical child
not knowing
expelliarmus
from x-ray the
drill salesman
and wife fully
aware locked
their charge to
the surface of
knowinglessness
but then
the wife had written
begging to join her
sister on that train
the dentists perfectly
content to be dentists
took their daughter
to Diagon Alley not
rejecting who she
was through who
they weren't.

Once Held

A lifelong seeker,
imagine my surprise
I'd been doing it wrong
diving and ascending
and diving again when
all I had to do was hover
still and attentive then
the golden tease would
present itself to me and
off I'd go
         at first
took a lifetime of beatings
bludgers quaffling chasing
rarely keepered before
the sought bestowed itself
of itself *Effortless Effort*
the letters glowed *Compassionate*
Non-Attachment to Outcome
scoreless the winged globe
opened showing why schools
jobs houses competitions
ministries called its secret
"Snitch." once held, games
over.

Choose

The wand chooses
the wizard it's not
always clear why
but I think I know
it's the same reason
we don't recall our
past lives (unaided)
or foresee next Tuesday
or understand prophecies
imagine if we remembered
tomorrows, what of oversized
chess games and dives for
swords? If Malfoys knew
they'd once been Muggles,
would Draco have been the
Chosen One? And with
prophecies clear as bells
who'd need remembrall's
student? No, the end
chooses the means;
had Harry seen his, surely
he'd have picked one of
those bazooka wands,
not the twin to You Know
Who's?

Horrorcrutches

It certainly wasn't
on purpose or for
immortality quite
the opposite we
only slid into our
hiding places wanting
to live less not more
to diminish, to avoid
crystal cups and blue
red flame we divided
our souls
stuffed them
where nobody else would
find us not even us the
most benign innocuous
confinements were our
horrorcrutches a sweet
smile unraised hand an
inoffensive ordinariness
oh but the price was the
same: an ended self
the one we might could
longed to become just
that much less than we
feared our own amplitude
we murdered our magic
by suffocation or so we
thought someone hunted
our horror capsized our
crutch and sent us sprawling
into selfhood who would
do such a thing? What

magical creature snuck
past our *confundus* to
place their love in our
fragmented heart?

Sorted

We know the magic is
there just down the alley
just through the platform
we've sensed it all along
and we know it's dark
and dangerous not just
disney and pixar as
well as simply glorious
we touch our scars
the one birth gave us
and the ones you did
and count ourselves
lucky to sense the mystery
though we don't fool
ourselves no letter's coming
no Anglia flying to our rescue
still the soundtrack underscores
each day in our heads and
we'd rather this small
magic from this maddeningly
close distance than to join
the rest of you in eating
death

Return

Forget the Illuminati!
The young lady at
Lowe's says *I love*
your Gryffindor scarf!
World Governments?
Skull and Bones? The
deaf kid in the Dunkies
line signs that he likes
my mask with its round
glasses and lightning
bolt. I thumbs-up back!
Ours is the most pervasive
most powerful society of
all time the Communion of
Potterheads the Church of
the Golden Trio we're
everywhere and lives of
unbelonging disappear
I'm wearing Hogwarts socks!
my new kid sister squeals
Me, too! I plank my foot
up on the counter of
return.

About the Author

Wayne-Daniel Berard, PhD, is an educator, poet, writer, shaman, and sage. An adoptee and former Franciscan seminarian, his adoption search led to the discovery and embrace of his Jewishness. Wayne-Daniel is a Peace Chaplain, an interfaith clergy person, and former college chaplain. His chapbook, *The Man Who Remembered Heaven,* won the New Eden Award in 2003. He publishes broadly in poetry, fiction, and non-fiction, including *When Christians Were Jews (That Is Now),* subtitled *Recovering the Lost Jewishness of Christianity with the Gospel of Mark* (Cowley Publications, 2006), a novel, *The Retreatants* (Smashwords, 2012), a chapbook, *Christine Day, Love Poems* (Kittacuck Press 2016), and a novella, *Everything We Want* (Bloodstone Press, 2018). His latest published full-length works are in poetry, *The Realm of Blessing* (Unsolicited Press, 2020), and *Art of Enlightenment* (Kelsay Books, 2021), in mystery fiction, *Noa(h) and the Bark,* in short fiction *The Lives and Spiritual Time of C.I. Abramovich,* and in novella, *Fall of the Medes* (Alien Buddha Press 2021). He is the co-founding editor of *Soul-Lit,* an online journal of spiritual poetry (www.soul-lit.com). Wayne-Daniel lives in Mansfield, MA with his wife, The Lovely Christine.

Made in United States
North Haven, CT
10 May 2022

19042077R00024